D1577869

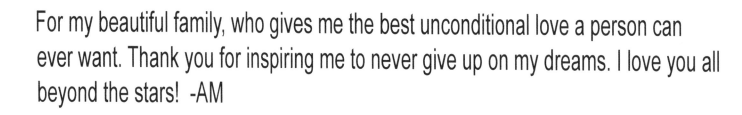

For my beautiful family, who gives me the best unconditional love a person can ever want. Thank you for inspiring me to never give up on my dreams. I love you all beyond the stars! -AM

ISBN-13: 978-0-692-10047-9

Gary
& the
Great
Inventors

Written by: Akura Marshall
Cover Design by: Al Joshua Spratling
Illustrations by: Adriel Meka

Hi! My name is Gary.

That's my twin brother Isaac and our friends,Tamara and Donté. We go waaaaaay back!

Isaac

TAMARA♡

Donté

We live in the great city of Washington, D.C. and there's lots of cool stuff to do here. We take pride in our city and we're always looking for ways to make it better.

Every Sunday, we take a trip to Mr. Baker's laundromat. He's a jolly old man who always smiles and gives us lots of treats!

"Honey, we need to go soon if we want to make it on time." That's my mother. She's a brainiac just like me! "Ok dear, I'm almost done." And that's my father, he's an engineer who makes all kinds of cool gadgets.

Gary's father puts the clothes in the trunk and his mother says, "Boys... It's time to go!" They hop in the car and wave goodbye to their friends.

When they arrive at Mr. Baker's shop, Gary spots a new sign in the window. "Hmmm... I wonder what that means," Gary thinks to himself.

"Why, hello! It's my favorite twins," says Mr. Baker.
"Hello," says the twins.

"My, my have you two grown since I last saw you," says Mr. Baker. The boys smile at each other and say,"we just saw you last week Mr. Baker, we haven't grown that much." Mr. Baker laughs as the boys enjoy their lollipops.

Gary points at the sign in the window and says, "What is organic dry cleaning?" Mr. Baker smiles and says, "All curious minds, right this way!" He signals for the boys to follow.

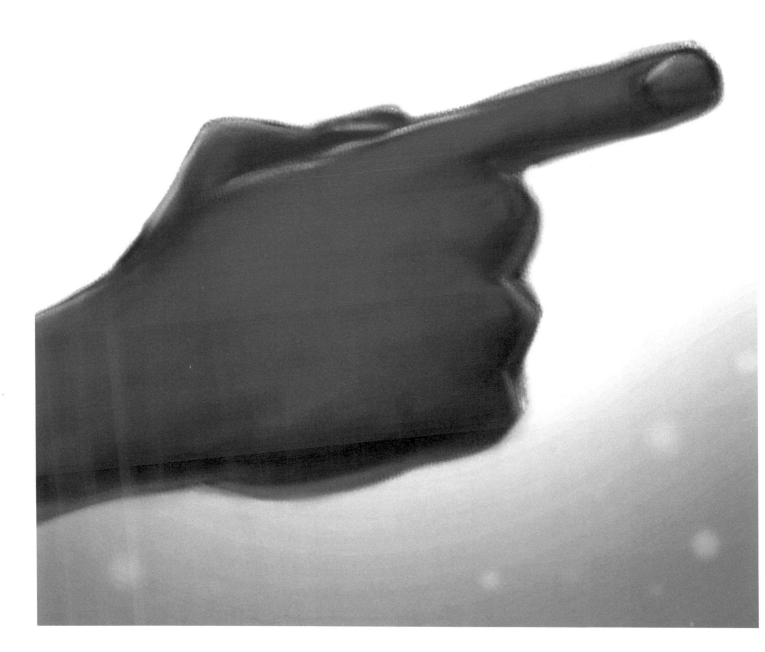

As they walk into a dark room, Mr. Baker turns the light on. To Gary's surprise he spots the biggest machine he has ever seen. "Coooool," says Gary. Mr. Baker smiles and says, "This is a dry cleaning machine. It cleans delicate clothing that cannot go into a normal washer or dryer."

U.S. Patent

Invention

Thomas Jennings

Mar. 3rd 1821

While Gary and Isaac check out the machine, Mr. Baker pulls out an old wilted piece of paper and passes it to Gary. It reads,

"Thomas Jennings, a reputable business owner, is the first African American to receive a United States patent for his dry-scouring method. This ruling generates controversy."

Gary stops and asks, "What is dry-scouring and why is it a controversy?" Mr. Baker smiles and says, "Young man all of the answers are right before you, keep reading." Gary smiles and reads on.

"At this time in America, the U.S. Patent Act of 1793 states that any invention an enslaved person makes belongs to their owner. However, Mr. Jennings, born a free man in 1791, meets the requirements to obtain a patent. Thus, becoming the first African American to receive full rights for his invention dry-scouring. This method revolutionizes the cleaning process of delicate garments."

"Wooooow, Mr. Jennings' story is amazing! I cannot believe his invention is so old and we still use it today," says Gary. "Why yes, and of course, there have been some upgrades along the way; however, Mr. Jennings and his blueprint will forever go down in our story," says Mr. Baker.

The boys rush back to help load the laundry in the car and say goodbye to Mr. Baker. On the way home, Gary stares out of the window and whispers,"One day I'm going to be a great inventor, just like Mr. Jennings."

The Beginning of
Something Great!!

GLOSSARY

Washington D.C.- the nation's capital, the center of politics, law making in America; and home to many museums, historical movements and monuments.

Laundromat- an establishment with coin-operated washing machines and dryers for public use.

Brainiac- an exceptionally intelligent person.

Inventor-a person who invented a particular process, device or who invents things as an occupation.

Gadgets- a small mechanical or electronic device or tool, especially an ingenious or novel one.

Organic- relating to or derived from living matter.

Delicate- very fine in texture or structure; of intricate workmanship or quality.

Wilted- become limp through heat, loss of water, or disease; droop.

Patent- a government authority or license conferring a right or title for a set period, especially the sole right to exclude others from making, using, or selling an invention.

Invents- create or design (something that has not existed before); be the originator of.

Reputation- the beliefs or opinions that are generally held about someone or something.

Custom- made or done to order for a particular customer.

Garments- an item of clothing.

Method- a particular form of procedure for accomplishing or approaching something

Controversy- disagreement, typically when prolonged, public, and heated.

Revolutionizes- change (something) radically or fundamentally.

Upgrades- raise (something) to a higher standard, in particular improve (equipment or machinery) by adding or replacing components (parts).

Blueprint- a design plan or other technical drawing.

About the Author

Akura Marshall was born in Anchorage, Alaska to a military family. She spent most of her childhood living in various cities in Germany. Her upbringing gave her a unique perspective on life; and most importantly, she learned the true value of culture and ancestoral connection. She is a mother of two children and an entreprenuer. Akura is passionate about re-connecting children to their roots and inspiring them to evoke the greatness from within. She has worked in the television industry for over 12 years and aspires to produce books and other content to reflect the true voice of children and families.

IG: Akura_M

About the Illustrator

Born in Montréal, Canada, 22-year-old Adriel is a recent graduate from the Savannah College of Art and Design.He possesses a professional background in illustration, a degree in Animation and, a minor in Industrial Design. Several of his works feature a consistent yet adaptive style with a variety of elements including animation, characters, traditional and digital art; product sketching and visual development. As for his work on Gary, Adriel worked with Akura to bring her vision for the story into reality and give all of the lovable characters their iconic images. From character designs, to sketches and iterations, all the way to final page paintings, once the artist's role was done he was able to use color visual storytelling to bring Gary and the gang soaring off of the pages!

Website: Adrielameka.wixsite.com/portfolio   IG: Arekusan_Meka

ArtStation: https://www.artstation.com/arekusan-meka

Youtube Channel: Our Children's Network
IG: @OurChildrensNetwork
FB.me/OurChildrensNetwork
Twitter: OurChildrensNet